IMAGES OF
Lowestoft

Eastern Daily Press

IMAGES OF
Lowestoft

The Breedon Books
Publishing Company
Derby

First published in Great Britain by
The Breedon Books Publishing Company Limited
Breedon House, 44 Friar Gate, Derby, DE1 1DA.
1996

Acknowledgements

Sincere thanks are due to former Eastern Counties Newspapers
staff photographer Alfred Lovett, whose work provided the great
majority of these images of Lowestoft and its people. He and the
other fine cameramen represented have created a fascinating
archive of times recently past. I am indebted to them all. My
thanks also to my wife Barbara, for her tolerance during the period
when research took precedence over an ordered domestic life.

ISBN 1 85983 047 1

Printed and bound by Butler & Tanner Ltd., Selwood Printing
Works, Caxton Road, Frome, Somerset.

Colour separations by Colour Services, Wigston, Leicester.

Jacket printed by Lawrence-Allen, Weston-Super-Mare, Avon.

Contents

Introduction

WHERE to begin? In the county of Suffolk there are many facets to the rich blend of history and tradition, farming and fishing, tourism and industry, which gives the area its unique appeal.

This is a land which has given birth to great artists and musicians, and provided inspiration for generations of builders and craftsmen. It is also a land which has nurtured a fine independence of spirit among a people who have long been accustomed to making shift for themselves.

Look around at what they have accomplished. The sturdy churches of the county bear witness to an impressive tradition of faith, and the farms and market towns and villages of Suffolk are testimony to the diligence of those who have gone before.

The North Sea which has shaped the eastern margins of the landscape for countless centuries has been by turns a bountiful friend and an implacable enemy, and its presence is always a force to be reckoned with by communities such as Lowestoft.

It is not, therefore, surprising that this book should also reflect the strong influence of the sea on everyday life in a busy port and holiday centre.

Photographers working for the *Eastern Daily Press* and its associated newspapers down the years have left a priceless record which shows the sea in all its moods.

They have braced themselves against the full fury of easterly gales in winter to picture the awesome power of white-capped breakers, and in the summer months have joined crowds of holidaymakers on award-winning local beaches to show the seaside in more benevolent mood.

Much of their work has also been concerned with the working life of the port, from the comings and goings of vessels in the fishing fleet to launching ceremonies and industrial and leisure developments around the harbour. Most of the pictures which appear in these pages were taken during the post-war years, from the 1950s onwards, and are well within the memory of thousands of people living in the town today. It is a measure of the pace of change in our society that so many of the scenes depicted have already acquired an historical significance.

The pattern of the fishing industry itself has changed in dramatic fashion. A modern enclosed market has replaced the open and increasingly inadequate quays where catches were landed and sold and processed for so many years. King Herring still ruled in the early 1950s, when the local drifter fleet was joined for the home voyage each autumn by Scottish vessels following the shoals on their migratory track around the coast.

But the industry had already become only a shadow of its former greatness, and within a few short years the drift-net fishery which had endured for centuries was no more. The drifters sailed into history and with them went all the traditions and ancillary occupations which were recorded in the nick of time by *Eastern Daily Press* photographers.

The departure of the drifters ushered in a period of dominance for the trawler fleet which made Lowestoft the premier plaice port in the United Kingdom. Even here, however, change has been constant. Traditional side-trawlers have now disappeared from the main local fleet, and after a period when stern trawling appeared to be the way forward, sophisticated beam trawlers have now taken over to dominate the harbour scene. They are fewer in numbers, and the quays are no longer crowded with fishing vessels, but the old magic remains whenever a trawler casts off and heads for the open sea.

The harbour skyline has changed in many other ways. The old North Extension has become the setting for a modern offshore construction yard building platforms for the oil and gas fields of the North Sea.

The pavilion which was built by Lowestoft Corporation on the South Pier in 1956 has been demolished and the area awaits new development to usher in the next century.

And a huge crane built on the South Quay to handle shipments of heavy components for the first Sizewell nuclear power station just along the coast was redundant and demolished before the completion of Sizewell B.

It has been a similar story of change elsewhere in the town. The former Beach Village area which housed so many fishing families has been swept away to be replaced by an industrial estate and become the home of the huge factories and cold stores of Birds Eye Wall's.

New roads have shifted traffic away from London Road North, which has become a pedestrian precinct. Town churches – including St John's to the south of the bridge and St Peter's to the north – have been knocked down to make way for housing developments. Gone too, is the Odeon Cinema, which has been replaced by a shopping centre.

Change has seen the arrival of new schools and new housing estates as Lowestoft has gradually extended its boundaries.

And Oulton Broad has been able to recapture something of the 'village' atmosphere of the past thanks to a new bridge and roadway which has shifted the flow of traffic and restored a human dimension to this popular waterside area.

Some of the industries which were once regarded as an essential part of the local economic structure have been casualties of change. The impact of worldwide recession has brought the closure of two major shipyards, Brooke Marine and Richards.

There have been other body blows with the closure of companies such as Eastern Coach Works and the Mortons and Co-op canning factories.

All these events, and more, have been brought into focus by the *Eastern Daily Press* team which has been on the spot to record events as they happened.

The art of the newspaper photographer, of course, extends far beyond coverage of the more dramatic incidents which capture the front page headlines.

Newspapers such as the *Eastern Daily Press* are an integral part of the community they serve, and many thousands of photographs have been taken down the years of ordinary people going about their ordinary occasions. People are the essential, ever-fascinating central ingredient of the content of every edition.

This book is inevitably an incomplete scrapbook of the countless events which have been covered in Lowestoft by the photographers who have submitted their work for publication.

Forty or so years ago, when Press photographers still used heavy plate cameras they knew that virtually every picture they took would appear in print. That can no longer be taken for granted in a world which has moved on apace. Picture editors of today are faced with an element of choice which was denied their predecessors.

What remains constant is the high quality of newspaper photography. The man with the camera is a professional working to tight deadlines, who is expected to get the best picture of any given event regardless of conditions. It has been a privilege to work down the years with so many *Eastern Daily Press* photographers who have been superb and dedicated craftsmen.

It has also been a privilege to explore the photographic archive and realise once again what a fine job has been done in capturing such incomparable images of a seaside town at work and play.

Trevor Westgate.
Lowestoft
Summer 1996

Wish You Were Here

The holiday scene in and around the town

THE irresistible combination of sea, sand and sunshine has delighted generations of visitors to the East Coast. Modern Lowestoft can offer much else besides, from the presence of Pleasurewood Hills Theme Park and the Suffolk Wildlife Park to specialist museums and an impressive range of annual events.

But traditional attractions will always draw thousands of families each summer to spend lazy days soaking up the sun, building castles in the sand and paddling in the shallows.

A stroll along the pier or prom is as much a part of a seaside holiday as watching the boats leave harbour. Small wonder that so many postcards are sent each year with the cheery message: "Having a lovely time. Wish you were here."

Crowded beaches in high summer are part of the memories of childhood we carry through life. What more can anyone ask than an opportunity to enjoy a day on a favourite beach. This is a scene on the popular South Beach in 1979.

And here is the beach alongside the Claremont Pier in the summer of 1975.

Throwing up ramparts against the advancing tide is part of the fun of building sandcastles, as these youngsters discovered at the end of July 1975.

All smiles at the water's edge when these local youngsters were taken to the beach to enjoy a burst of spring sunshine in May 1976.

Hunting for shrimps and starfish and seaweed in the shallows which provided a fascinating playground for these children near the South Pier in 1978.

Reaching for the sky. Swingboats on the South Beach at Lowestoft.

Young and old enjoying the beach sunshine.

That's the way to do it! Young members of the summer audience watching the Punch and Judy show on the South Beach.

The electric boats at Oulton Broad during the summer season of 1975.

The waterways at Kensington Gardens, a popular attraction for many years. But the electric boats are fading into memory now that the setting has become a pond devoted to model craft.

Youngsters having fun paddling their own canoes on the boating lake on Lowestoft seafront in 1978.

Come on in, the water's lovely. It was early April in 1980, but warm enough for these Lowestoft schoolchildren to enjoy a dip in the sea at Kirkley.

Another season, this time that of 1960, and the May temperature was chill enough for youngsters visiting the seafront playground to keep well wrapped up.

Everyone enjoys a splash in the sea at some time. Janie the elephant thoroughly enjoyed her daily dip when the Roberts Circus encamped on the North Denes, just a few yards from the beach, in 1976. Keeping a close eye on Janie is Bobby Roberts.

Family occasions as bathers take to the water off the South Beach in the 1980s.

The team of four 'Tuttles Tiny Tots' which won the prize for the most artistic sandcastle in a charity contest on the South Beach in the summer of 1980.

Having an absolutely smashing time. Piano-smashing competitions enjoyed a brief period of popularity in the early 1980s, before supplies ran out. Here is the start of an attempt by a women's team to break records. Wielding the sledgehammers are (left to right) Jane Whitehead, Yvonne Dziuram, Sue Deakin, Amanda Dickinson, Jennifer Reeve and Tina Cassidy.

Tours of the docks and fish market are always popular. Pictured here are pupils from Roman Hill Junior School on board a local trawler in 1977.

Holidaymakers watching a trawl net being mended during a guided tour of the harbour in 1976. The expert commentary is being given by Skipper Arthur Brinded (extreme left).

The resident ducks and swans at Oulton Broad have become expert in scrounging scraps of bread from holidaymakers. This scene at the Yacht Station shows the crew of the cruiser *Janet V* feeding the swans in 1978.

Enterprises sailing in close array at Oulton Broad in 1969.

A flotilla of canoeists passing through Mutford Lock in 1963.

Horses from a local riding school being exercised on the long stretch of open dunes between Pakefield and Kessingland in the warm autumn sunshine in October 1980.

Young anglers hoping to make a good catch at Oulton Broad in the summer of 1976.

Spectators on the South Pier watching the Dragons preparing for another day's racing at sea.

Dragon yachts hoisting sails to compete in the Lowestoft Sea Week races of 1965. The comings and goings around the Yacht Basin always attract plenty of interest among holidaymakers.

Crowded waters and crowded vantage points along the edge of Nicholas Everitt Park at Oulton Broad in June 1964.

The South Beach at Lowestoft pictured from the top of the 60ft South Pier Pavilion tower in the early 1960s. The pavilion has since been demolished.

A pleasure steamer passing through Mutford Lock at Oulton Broad.

The Esplanade Boating Lake at Lowestoft in 1958.

The seafront miniature railway was a popular attraction for many years. This picture was taken on Whit Monday, 1959.

Helping hands. No shortage of volunteers to help push out the boat from the South Beach in 1959.

Young visitors to Lowestoft lighthouse, one of the oldest established permanent lights around the coast, in 1977.

Tents dominated the scene on the North Denes at Lowestoft when this picture was taken in 1959. Today the summer scene is dominated by the presence of touring and permanent caravans.

A pair of thoroughbreds. Dragon yachts entering harbour after competing in the Edinburgh Cup series in 1966. On the right is race winner *Polly K11* (J.D.Howden Hume). Alongside is *Indros* (R.O.Bond), which finished seventh.

Boat hirers awaiting customers on the Boulevard at Oulton Broad Yacht Station in 1964.

Sports boats racing at Oulton Broad to entertain a large crowd during the regatta week meeting in August 1975.

An Enterprise dinghy being driven hard through a squall when strong winds provided some lively sailing in the Waveney and Oulton Broad Yacht Club's three-day Easter open regatta in 1981.

The Regimental Band and Corps of Drums of the 1st Battalion, the Royal Anglian Regiment, beating Retreat on Royal Plain in the summer of 1966. In the foreground is the civic party headed by the Mayor, Roy Burgess, who took the salute.

This Working Life

The business of earning a living

THERE has been a painful adjustment to changed economic conditions and social patterns within many traditional industries in the Lowestoft area in recent years. Gone are the days when a young apprentice could look forward with some certainty to a working life at the same shipyard or factory.

Decades of tradition have been swept away with the closure of a number of long established companies, and the consequent loss of many hundreds of skilled jobs.

New developments have as yet failed to fill the breach in terms of jobs or the general level of economic prosperity, and dormant skills await an opportunity to demonstrate once more local pride in a job well done.

Some facets of Lowestoft working life shown in this selection remain little changed. Others have slipped into a fondly remembered past.

Frozen moment. A 3cwt block of clear ice, fresh from the mould, at the Lowestoft Ice Company in 1981.

Bill Whatley, general secretary of the Union of Shop, Distributive and Allied Workers, pausing to sample some tinned fruit with the quality inspectors during a tour of the former CWS canning factory in 1982.

Sludge being pumped from one of the gas-holders which were once a prominent feature of the local scene, and were demolished in 1975.

Painting the lights at the harbour entrance in the summer of 1966.

The ability to make a strong net, like that of riding a bike, is never forgotten once acquired. These former fishermen, pictured at J.W.Stuart's premises in Star Buildings in 1966, had between them spent more than 170 years at sea. They were (from left) George Cone, James Nickerson, Bob 'Colls' Durrant and Charles 'Dip' Lincoln.

Hundreds of local women once worked as beatsters, repairing the miles of nets needed by the local drifter fleet. By the mid-1960s the dwindling fleet meant that another skilled trade was dying out. These workers were employed by the Blackcat Fishing Company.

Caulking the seams of the wherry *Albion* on the slipway at Lowestoft in 1978.

It was in the era before the discovery of natural gas supplies beneath the North Sea, and the Lowestoft Gas Works was still in production. Staff at the works are seen here facing the camera in 1959.

Another vessel in the dry dock for repairs, this time in 1970.

Circuit panels for colour televisions being assembled at the former factory of TV Manufacturing Ltd in 1968.

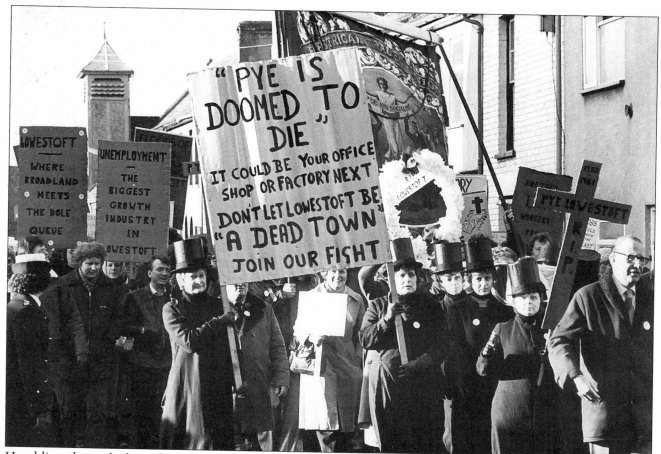

Heralding the end of another local company. Workers at the Pye factory voice their fears over the impact of closure during a protest march in 1980.

No, not a scene in a local church belfry but the start of operations at Lowestoft's new telephone exchange in 1961.

Lowestoft firemen relaxing with a welcome mug of tea after bringing a blaze at the long disused Cozy Corner cinema under control in September 1960.

George Ford (left) and his brother, Jim, at work at the bottom of a tunnel shaft at Lowestoft during the course of installing a new main drainage system for the town.

Boats galore. The production line at the Yarecraft factory which was busy in the town in the early 1960s.

A Corporation gardener at work in the Katwijk garden named after the town's 'twin' in Holland. The picture was taken in 1963. The garden alongside Lowestoft lighthouse flourishes to the present day.

Workmen breaking up ice on Leathes' Ham to ease drainage into nearby Lake Lothing towards the end of a severe winter in March 1963.

Destination Baghdad. One of hundreds of buses turned out by the craftsmen of the former Eastern Coach Works plant at Lowestoft. This contract was in 1986.

The last bus nearing completion at Eastern Coach Works in 1987.

Putting the finishing touches to the interior of another bus.

The carpenters' shop at the Lowestoft Corporation Depot in 1970. Men working here produced the joinery for hundreds of local homes.

Signs of the times. The paint shop at the Corporation Depot.

The Corporation's vehicle repair shop, providing another glimpse of the wide range of services taken for granted as part of the work of a local authority.

The blacksmith's shop where Corporation craftsmen turned their hands to a variety of tasks.

Long service awards being presented to estate workers by Lord Somerleyton (right) at Somerleyton Hall in 1970.

Union leader Jack Jones (second from left) watching fish cakes going into a cooking machine during a tour of the Birds Eye factory at Lowestoft in 1976.

The flags were out in the body shop at Eastern Coach Works in 1976 when Edward Plant retired after 51 years with the company. He is pictured surrounded by his workmates as the tankard they gave him was filled for a celebration drink by body shop foreman John Gardiner.

A guide explaining the work done at the Pye television factory during an open day which attracted over 500 visitors in 1976.

Docks Board workmen winching open the town's old swing bridge after its ultimate breakdown in 1968.

All in a day's work. A practice torpedo picked up by the Lowestoft inshore trawler *Sweet Waters* being lifted ashore in the Hamilton Dock in 1977.

And the real thing. Members of the Portsmouth and Medway Clearance Diving Team with a 200lb depth charge which they exploded on the beach at Benacre in 1977.

Up she goes. A dense column of shingle, topped by a cloud of black smoke, erupts from the beach as the depth charge is detonated.

A day to remember. Tram service veterans were invited to the East Anglia Transport Museum at Carlton Colville in 1964 to see some of the old-time vehicles.

Not a computer screen in sight. An audio-visual typing course in progress in the Commerce Department of the new Lowestoft College in 1965.

Students in the College panel beating class working under the watchful eye of the instructor, Mr W.D.Hulme, in the building department.

Part-time Civil Defence workers putting the finishing touches to one of the field kitchens they built at Rogerson Hall, Corton, during a two-day exercise in 1965.

Lowestoft Corporation sea defence workers keeping watch on a 65ft pile being driven into the beach near Children's Corner. It was start of work in 1965 on a 250ft long wall of sheet piling to protect this stretch of the esplanade.

This huge 200-ton crane was built on the South Quay in 1962 to handle loads for the Sizewell nuclear power station. Among the consignments was this 50-ton boiler section.

Looking like a set of giant organ pipes, these cyclone collectors were perched on top of the 65ft plant installed at the new Boulton and Paul factory in 1962 to extract dust and wood waste from air drawn from the main factory.

Young visitors to a Careers '77 exhibition at Lowestoft College learning how artists' brushes are made at the Windsor & Newton stand. Over 20 stands showed local school leavers a wide range of jobs open to them in an era when work was easier to find.

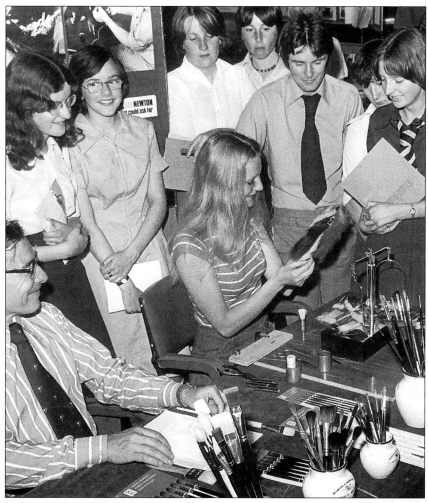

Schoolgirls watching part of the work that goes into making a fashion shoe on the Bally's stand at the careers exhibition.

Rebuilding work at the Oulton Broad yacht station in progress in 1970.

Don't forget the diver. Work in progress beneath the surface of Lowestoft harbour attracts an interested audience in the summer of 1960.

The Show Goes On

Summer theatre and other productions

SUMMER shows and midwinter pantomimes are all part of the traditional pattern of entertainment in a seaside town such as Lowestoft.

The town's old Sparrow's Nest Theatre, which was at the core of civic entertainment for many years, is no more. Its place has been taken by the handsomely restored Marina Theatre in the centre of the town.

The South Pier Pavilion has also been demolished, and with it has gone another centre for live entertainment. But the shows go on, with unabated zest. Visiting professional companies give a glimpse of the glamorous life of the West End stage and there is a flourishing amateur tradition which allows many talented local performers to appear in the stage spotlight.

There are countless school productions during the course of a year, and the tiny Seagull Theatre in South Lowestoft is the setting for other-stage presentations.

The curtain is rung up here on some of the popular presentations enjoyed by local audiences in recent years.

On the stroke of midnight Cinderella (Elizabeth Reader-Parkes) runs from the ballroom to the dismay of Prince Charming (Olynne Underwood) a scene from the Lowestoft Players' pantomime at Sparrow's Nest Theatre in January 1969.

Another moment of fairytale magic from the 1969 production of *Cinderella*.

Have at thee, varlet! The grassed lawns surrounding Gunton Hall at Lowestoft became a battlefield when knights from the Norwich & Norfolk Mediaeval Society presented a tournament as part of the attractions during the Lowestoft Homes and Trades Fair in 1981.

The mediaeval theme was also pursued, in a more peaceful fashion, at this midsummer fair organised by the Blundeston School Association in the summer of 1978.

Carnival time is always one of the major highlights of the summer season, and the Lowestoft procession is one of the largest of its kind in the region. This impressive three-headed monster won a first prize for Lowestoft Players in 1979.

Dancing clowns did their bit to boost the spirit of carnival during that same summer of 1979.

In 1981 the carnival procession prizewinners included this entry from the Telecoms sports and social club.

And there was a reminder of the Royal wedding in this decorated car entry.

A great deal of ingenuity and hard work goes into preparations for the big carnival day. And in a seaside town such as Lowestoft it isn't surprising that there should often be a maritime theme, as there was in this entry in 1964.

A stylish carriage with a heartfelt message, as Rosina Jennings waves to passers-by in the 1980 carnival.

Howdy pardners. A glimpse of the Wild West in the 1980 procession.

Funds collected during the carnival go to help patients in the Lowestoft and North Suffolk Hospital and by the end of the route a bucket of small coins can be quite a weighty load.

Another colourful entry from the 1980 carnival, this time an invitation to travel to distant horizons from the Seaforths travel agency.

One of the big television attractions of the time was the *Black and White Minstrel Show*. And the theme was taken up by Warners Holiday Camp to provide inspiration for a carnival entry in 1965. The giant figure took eight weeks to build and more than 150 people staying at the camp took part in the procession through the town.

The age of space travel encouraged local designers to come up with their own version of home-made rocket technology in the summer of 1965.

Lowestoft's notoriously fickle swing bridge then nearing the end of its working life provoked this suggestion for a replacement opening mechanism, in the 1969 carnival.

BRIDGE CLOSED EVERY DRY MONDAY 8.30 a.m.

Staff at the Lowestoft Fisheries Laboratory in a typically light-hearted contribution to the carnival fun and games in 1965.

No prizes for guessing the name of the production. It was, of course, *Puss in Boots*, presented by Lowestoft Players at the Sparrow's Nest Theatre in 1976. In the foreground are Jack (Stephen Wilson) with principal boy Tom (Sally Ennew) and her cat (Avril Randall).

Visiting summer show star Jack Tripp shows his horsemanship skills at the St Peter's and St John's summer fete in 1976.

The Lisa Gaye Dancers and the star of the show, Bernie Clifton, at rehearsals for the the summer season at Sparrow's Nest Theatre in 1977.

The lineup of performers in the Sparrow's Nest summer show in 1967.

Another visiting show business personality, the much-loved Frankie Howerd, opening the Lothingland Hospital fete during the 1970s.

Comedian Ernest Arnley, co-star Gloria Day, and the Eight Starlettes in an Egyptian scene from Lowestoft's summer show, *Starlight Rendezvous*, at Sparrow's Nest in 1965.

The chorus of Holiday Spectacular in their ostrich-plumed costumes for the opening of the summer show at Sparrow's Nest in 1979.

The South Pier Pavilion show lineup in 1966.

Lothingland School Band making music in concert in 1966.

The Harris School choir in good voice in 1966.

The Dell Primary School choir taking part in the Beccles Music Festival in the spring of 1966.

A performance by the choir of Briar Clyffe School, which was established in the Gunton Cliff home once owned by London store magnate Howard Hollingsworth, a major benefactor to the town.

A section of the North Suffolk Youth Wind Orchestra, pictured in 1977.

A scene on the quarter-deck of *HMS Pinafore* as the Denes High School presented their Christmas production in 1970.

High drama on stage during the Lowestoft College Theatre Group's production of the third act from *Julius Caesar* at the Suffolk Drama Festival in 1963.

Rehearsals for the Lowestoft Choral Society production of *Tom Jones* in 1950.

About to reach a wide audience but without appearing in the spotlight are these bellringers at St Peter's Church, Carlton Colville.

A scene from the spectacular production of *Showboat*, staged by Lowestoft Players at Sparrow's Nest Theatre in 1975.

Annie Oakley (Deanne Dickson) meets her sharpshooting rival Frank Butler (John Millward) in the first scene of the Lowestoft Players production of *Annie Get Your Gun*, at the Sparrow's Nest Theatre in 1977.

Enchanting young dancers join Wishee Washee (Stephen Wilson) in a song from the Lowestoft Players pantomime *Aladdin* at the Sparrow's Nest Theatre in 1978.

Widow Twankey (Terry Rymer) enjoying his visit to the 'royal baths' with the ladies of the court in the 1978 pantomime.

The quarrelsome Ugly Sisters (Lee Risebrow, right) and Ron Morley, arguing with the Baron in a production of *Cinderella* in 1975.

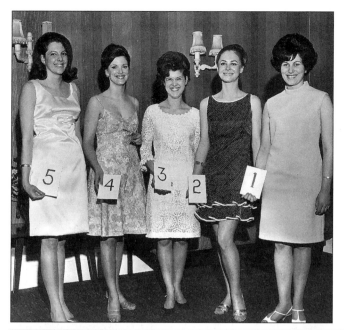

The five football queens who took part in the contest for the title of Eastern Area Football Queen at the Hotel Victoria in 1967. The winner was Miss Harwich and Parkeston, Janice Payne, on the extreme right of the picture, with Miss Lowestoft, Gillian Barton, second from left, as runner-up.

Not a stage show, but a production of some magnitude nonetheless. This was the jubilee market organised at the Harris School in 1977.

And here is another very special occasion, the Coronation Day street party held in 1953 for children of the Beach area of Lowestoft.

And here is another highly popular open air event which has become part and parcel of the life of Lowestoft. It shows the annual Petticoat Lane charity event organised by members of Lowestoft Lions Club. The setting in 1969 was Commercial Road.

People In Focus

Moments from local lives

PEOPLE are put into focus in every issue of a regional newspaper. Personal occasions make the news as people celebrate milestones along their journey through life.

In some respects the yearly round follows a traditional pattern, from springtime to harvest, though there are apt to be newcomers on each occasion when the camera calls on school or village or domestic scene.

Some individuals within the community are destined to become well-known characters while others make only a relatively fleeting appearance in the public eye.

All have a distinctive contribution to make to the area in which they live and work.

Here are some of the men and women, and children, of our town.

Children at Dell Primary School with their harvest festival display in the autumn of 1966.

Turning back the clock. A display of 19th-century fashions at the reception held in 1973 to mark the centenary of the *Lowestoft Journal* weekly newspaper.

Lowestoft historian Jack Rose – a self-taught expert on past times in the town who has a rich fund of stories to tell during his popular lectures. He is the founder of a memorial museum dedicated to all the local people who served in any capacity during World War Two.

The opening of the Waveney Sports and Leisure Centre at Lowestoft in 1981 coincided with Daphne Mellor's term in office as chairman of Waveney District Council. Never a stickler for formality, she promptly went behind the bar to pull the first pint.

The late Tommy Turrell was a familiar figure for many years in the annual Lowestoft Carnival procession. His joy was always apparent as he waved to passers-by along the route, and photographers always made a point of recording his distinctive contribution to the local scene.

Somerleyton blacksmith Billy Horner with the shield presented to him by Lord and Lady Somerleyton in 1976 to mark his retirement after 50 years on the estate. The horseshoe mounted on the shield was made by Mr Horner for Lady Somerleyton's horse Honeybrook, the winner of many point to point races.

Centenarian Horace Bull about to set off for a day's fishing off the port aboard the *Dollybird* in 1977. He was accompanied by boatman Bob Williams.

Waveney planning officer Laurence Monkhouse with the original model of the statue *Call of the Sea* which stands in Station Square. Now an accepted part of the local scene, the design of the statue caused some controversy when it was unveiled in 1981.

Dredging of the River Hundred in 1981 produced relics of the prehistoric past in the shape of a pair of impressive ox horns. Holding the relics are Anglian Water Authority workers Peter Plant and Keith Woods.

The title of Lowestoft and District Winemaker of the Year was won for the third time in 1978 by Beryl Rooke, pictured here with some of the ingredients needed to make her the toast of the town.

Birds of the wild often come unexpectedly to hand in a town such as Lowestoft. This injured kestrel was cared for in 1982 by local man David Rampling.

Local MP Jim Prior, who was Northern Ireland Secretary when this picture was taken in the early 1980s, is seen talking with the president of the Trawl Fish Merchants' Association, Mr B.E.Bemment (in white coat), and the Association secretary, George Howard, during an early morning visit to the fish market.

Twelve-year-old Simon Friston of Carlton Colville with the town's most famous tortoise, Ali Pasha, in 1980. The tortoise was brought back from the Gallipoli landings in 1916 by his grandfather, Henry Friston.

Each year on the feast of St Valentine on 14 February, village children visit Somerleyton Hall to be presented with sticky buns. The tradition has gone on for at least a century, and in 1980 these youngsters dressed for the occasion as their Victorian forbears would have done.

Artist Francis Paesbrugghe, a native of Belgium, made his home in Lowestoft after serving with the Brigade Piron during World War Two. A specialist in wool tapestry pictures, he presented a number of his works to members of the Royal Family. This one was accepted by the Queen.

The china industry which briefly flourished at Lowestoft two centuries ago has provided a precious legacy for admirers and collectors of the rare and beautiful. Librarian Victor Steward is seen here in 1966 holding a decorated bowl with blue bands and flowers which was designed by one of the founders of the Lowestoft factory, Robert Browne.

General dealer Jack Cleveland, a familiar figure with his homburg hat and bow tie in local auction rooms for many years, always remembered the needs of old people. Here he is in 1965 making the rounds delivering a Christmas parcel to 95-year-old Mary Read. With him is his son Peter Cleveland and six-year-old Nicola Cleveland.

Survival techniques can be vital in the warmer days of summer. This picture of Lowestoft Lifeguard Corps carrying out a rescue drill in 1980 was taken in the August sunshine on the South Beach.

Making a splash in the harbour in January. Trainees on a Lowestoft offshore survival course in 1982 get instructions on the quayside of the Yacht Basin. Then they put theory into practice by jumping into the icy water and swimming around in a circle. They were expected to sing *Ten Green Bottles* while paddling as a means of keeping their spirits up.

Lest we forget. War veterans standing to attention as *Last Post* is sounded at the Remembrance Sunday Service at the Lowestoft War Memorial on Royal Plain. The year was 1965.

Veterans of campaigns around the world. Chelsea Pensioners enjoying a stay at the seaside at the Lord Kitchener Memorial Holiday Centre for ex-Servicemen and women. The centre continues to flourish, and pensioners from Chelsea are regular visitors each summer.

Marshman Tom Crawford shows off his pet coypu, Joe, to Somerleyton neighbour Mrs L. Ansdell and her two-year-old granddaughter Debbie. The year was 1965 and the campaign which eradicated coypu from Broadland was still some way in the future.

Sightseers gather around Anglia TV newscaster Colin Bower and his bride, 18-year-old Jill Edwards, a former Miss Lowestoft, as they left Pakefield Church in March 1963.

Stan Newby, pictured in 1977 with the curfew bell which is still rung each evening at Lowestoft Town Hall. The nightly curfew is said to have started following a major fire which swept through much of the town in the 17th century. It is rung at 8pm each weekday evening.

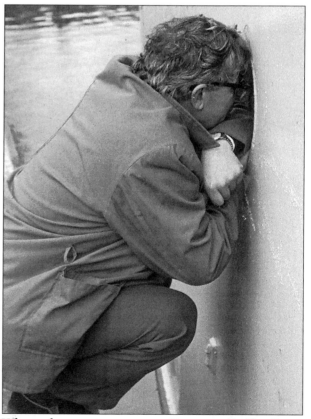

Lowestoft fish merchant Arthur Evans with his straw 'titfer' on the market in 1977.

What the reporter saw. *Eastern Daily Press* journalist Peter Cherry pictured unawares in the late 1970s as he chatted to a stowaway through the porthole of a ship berthed in the harbour.

Aubrey Moore, president of the Lowestoft Fishing Vessel Owners' Association (left), explains the finer points of a freshly landed plaice to Fisheries Minister Edward Bishop in the summer of 1976.

Retired Lowestoft boatbuilder Frank Jowett travelled the world to collect these exotic shells. He was pictured with his collection in 1981.

Far left: Edmonton's 69-year-old Pearly King, Jimmy Turner, brought his fund-raising talents to town in 1965 when he spent a week collecting cash on behalf of the Lord Kitchener Memorial Holiday Centre.

Left: Man of Broadland. Oulton Broad harbour master Bill Soloman pictured on the stretch of water he loved during the summer of 1976. Every inch the sailor, Bill had a collection of yarns about ghostly waterborne legends guaranteed to turn a gullible visitor goggle-eyed.

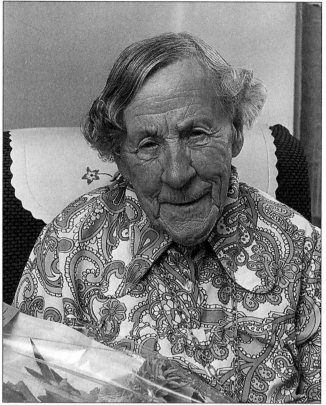

Longevity is something of an East Anglian characteristic, it being reckoned that anyone who can survive a winter on this exposed coast is well equipped to continue doing so for years to come. Emma Cook, pictured here on her 101st birthday in 1976, celebrated with a visit to Bressingham Gardens.

Mind my bike! Pc Michael Worley setting off on cycle patrol from Lowestoft Police Station in 1977.

And here is the most remarkable Lowestoft centenarian of them all. Ada Roe, pictured after casting her vote in 1966, ran her dairy in Clapham Road for decades and was known as the country's oldest shopkeeper. She eventually died on 11 January 1970, just a month before her 112th birthday.

Park keeper Tony Carpenter and his alsatian Chinta in Nicholas Everitt Park, Oulton Broad in 1976.

All at sea? Not quite. This drifter cabin is an exact replica, built at the Lowestoft and East Suffolk Maritime Society museum at Sparrow's Nest, Lowestoft and guaranteed not to roll and pitch in a storm. Pictured here in 1980 are Society secretary Ralph Mitchell (seated) and Ernest Pye scraping the deck.

One of the most doughty campaigners against the system of paying church tithes on land was farmer Albert Mobbs, who fought many a legal battle. He is seen here in the tranquil setting of his home at Oulton.

Break of day. Workmen with the cockerel weathervane from the spire of St John's Church, which became redundant and was demolished to make way for a housing scheme in 1978.

And another cockerel which still proudly greets the rising sun each morning. The gilded cock which tops the 120ft spire of St Margaret's Parish Church is seen being fixed in place by Mr R.Taylor following renovation work to the spire in 1954.

Veteran yachtswoman Lady Mayhew showing her granddaughter, Miss Margaret Harvey, the giant cake presented to her at the annual dinner of the Broads One Design Class at the Royal Norfolk & Suffolk Yacht Club in 1977.

Driver William George took the last train on the run from Great Yarmouth Southtown station to Lowestoft Central when the coastal line was closed in May 1970.

That's the way to do it! Mr Punch gets a final spot of paint on his famous nose, ready for the coming season in 1976. Repainting the puppets, some of them a century old, is Punch and Judy man Harold Woolnough.

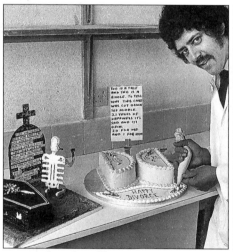

Cakes for all occasions – for birthdays, anniversaries and for divorces and funerals. Confectioner Brian Morrison pipes in the broken hearts for a special divorce cake at Bushell's Bakery in 1976.

It was a golden summer in the garden. And Reg Gower made the most of it in 1976 when he produced this magnificent cucumber, weighing a staggering 5lb 9½oz, in his small greenhouse at Woods Loke East.

Full-time eel catcher William 'Deafy' Moore netted many thousands of eels during his working life. But when this picture was taken of him at work in 1962 he admitted that he had never fancied eating one.

John Dunne giving a helping hand to a youngster planting a rowan tree at St Mary's school to mark the Queen's Silver Jubilee in 1977.

The Harbour Scene

The maritime hub of industry and leisure alike

THE harbour at Lowestoft owes more to Victorian enterprise than to nature, and it was only in the 1830s that works were begun to create a waterway extending from the new port to Norwich.

The present inner harbour, known as Lake Lothing, was formerly a freshwater lake, but the new passage to the sea marked the real beginning of substantial ship-building and ancillary industries and gave impetus to the rapid growth of the town.

The man who transformed the town was the energetic Sir Samuel Morton Peto, who pushed through not only the railway and harbour works essential to economic development, but also embarked upon the building of the Esplanade, Marine Parade and associated projects.

The intervening years have seen the rise and subsequent decline of industries which have made the name of Lowestoft known across the world for quality products and good craftsmanship.

The collapse of the shipbuilding industry has claimed two major local yards, Brooke Marine and Richards, and their passing and that of other victims of recession has marked the end of a remarkable era.

There have also been new beginnings, not least with important links between the port and the exploration programme for oil and gas deposits beneath the North Sea.

Container ships and modern terminals have replaced the labour intensive methods of the past, and Lowestoft has shown a healthy ability to adapt to changing times.

The harbour remains the centre of a vigorous community.

Spectators on the pierhead watching the pirate radio vessel *Caroline* enter harbour in 1966 after spending the night anchored in Lowestoft Roads. Repairs were carried out to *Caroline's* hull at the Richards' shipyard.

A moment of drama on the quayside when a crane toppled and smashed into the Lowestoft pilot boat in 1980.

Another mishap took place in 1976, when a Waveney District Council lorry landed on the beach near the North Denes caravan site.

Fisherman William Crago (right) and his crewman Roger Doy, with an aircraft propeller trawled up off Corton in 1977. Relics of the last war are still being recovered from the bed of the North Sea.

A massive rig module being moved into position ready to be inched on board a giant barge at Lowestoft in 1980.

The barge *Hajos Turtle*, carrying a 1,500 tonne rig module, squeezes through the bridge channel at Lowestoft. The module was destined for the *Shell Fulmar A* platform in the North Sea.

Royal tour: The Duke of Edinburgh, accompanied by Brooke Marine shipyard chairman Harry Dowsett, during a tour of the yard in 1967.

Women workers at the neighbouring TV Manufacturing Ltd factory had a cheery wave for the Duke when he arrived at the Brooke Marine yard.

The Duke talking to Brooke Marine platers.

Princess Alice, Duchess of Gloucester, watching the vessel she had just named, the *HMAV Ardennes*, go down the slipway at the Brooke Marine yard in 1976. With her is the yard chairman, Harry Dowsett.

Princess Alice talking to spectators at the launch.

The 295ft chemical tanker *Skeldergate*, the largest vessel then built at the Richard's shipyard, being assisted out of harbour for her final sea trials in 1976.

This 33 metre, fast patrol craft, *Hadejia*, was one of a pair of Nigerian Navy warships which returned in 1981 to the Brooke Marine yard for a refit.

A network of cranes on the South Quay in February 1976.

Too large to enter the harbour, the frigate *HMS Lowestoft* dropped anchor off her name port when she paid an official visit in May 1967.

An air-sea rescue helicopter from RAF Coltishall hovers low above the port lifeboat to transfer a 'survivor' during the annual lifeboat day exercise.

With the crew safely aboard, a glass-fibre capsule is winched down into the waters of Oulton Broad during a survival training course in 1976.

Champagne occasion. Miss Monica Eades names the new tug *Kelty* at the Richards shipyard in 1976.

The 195ft molasses tanker *Athelbrook* being towed into a fitting out berth after her launching at the Richard's yard in 1976.

Flags flying aboard the new stern trawler *Barnby Queen*, which joined the Lowestoft fishing fleet in 1976.

A reminder of the gracious days of sail. The top-sail schooner *Lindo* which visited Lowestoft harbour in 1977.

The launch by crane of the ferry *Triton* at the Brooke Marine yard in 1960.

Dry dock. Painters at work on the trawler *Boston Victor*, with the *Boston Provost* awaiting her turn for the same treatment in 1967.

The Union Jack is unfurled on the bows of the l90ft coastal survey vessel HMS *Bulldog*, as she slides smoothly down the slipway at her launching from the Brooke Marine shipyard in 1967.

The Russian trawler *Kotlas* taking to the water after her launch at the Brooke Marine yard in 1957.

The Lowestoft dredger *Lake Lothing* had an unusual role in 1956 when she was chosen as the setting for the BBC radio programme, *Down to the Sea*, in 1956.

Work in progress on new quay headings for the Ministry of Fisheries research vessels in 1967.

The huge crane which was built on the South Quay at Lowestoft to handle shipments of major items for the Sizewell A nuclear power station.

Hundreds of people flocked to the Trawl Dock for a rare opportunity to go aboard a Royal Navy submarine paying a visit to the port in 1951.

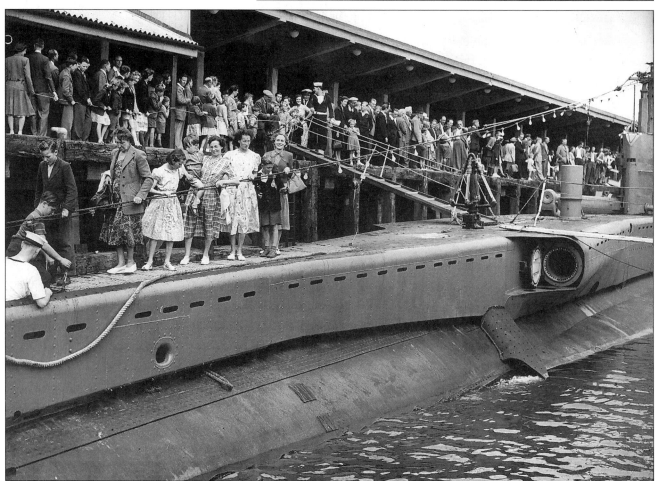

A timber shipment being discharged at the Boulton & Paul yard alongside *Lake Lothing* in 1969.

After carrying out a seven-month oil survey in the North Sea, these two survey ships, the *Clearwater*, of Dublin, and the *Bayou Chico*, of Pascagoula, called in at Lowestoft for a few days in 1964.

Liquid mud gushing out from around the drilling pipes on board the rig *Neptune 1*, some 65 miles north-east of the servicing base at Lowestoft in 1965.

Looking across the deck of *Neptune 1* to the helicopter landing platform in 1965.

Pile driving in progress on the site of the new £920,000 Boulton & Paul timber factory in 1961. An 800ft quay was built to serve the development.

The drilling rig *Neptune 1*.

And the band played on. The commissioning service for the survey ship *HMS Fawn* at the Brooke Marine shipyard in 1968.

The work of fitting out the 303ft passenger cargo ship *Bolton Abbey* at the Brooke Marine shipyard in 1958.

A strike at the Brooke Marine shipyard in 1970 prevented the launch of the trawler *Ranger Cadmus*. But the ship was named by Lady Harmer, pictured here leaving the platform with Harry Dowsett, head of the shipyard.

Another major boost to the growing interest being taken by British farmers in French Charolais cattle came with the arrival at Lowestoft in 1970 of a consignment of 288 heifers and 25 bulls from Brest and Le Havre. The cattle arrived on board the *MV Eemsmond* and spent four weeks in quarantine before being sent to farms all over the country.

The powerful screws of the tug *Keston* seen to advantage on the slipway in 1970.

The Lowestoft trawler *Grenada* in dry dock for inspection and repairs following her stranding on Hopton beach at the end of 1969.

Walking on water? Not quite. But it looked that way as a sailor fixed the ship's boarding ladder on the side of the frigate *HMS Lowestoft* in preparation for visitors in 1979.

The skyline of Lowestoft was changed when this giant top section of a gas production platform arrived from Middlesbrough in 1977. Towering over the Hamilton Dock, the section was completed at Lowestoft before becoming part of Shell's *Indefatigable L* platform.

The launch of the *USS Edenton* at Brooke Marine in 1968.

Another new trawler for the Lowestoft fleet, the 116ft diesel vessel *Carlton Queen*, slides down the slipway at Brooke Marine in 1961. She was built for Talisman Trawlers. The launching mistress was Mrs C.W.Scott, niece of the chairman of the owning company, Mr J.E.Guthe.

The Lowestoft trawler *Boston Viscount* undergoing an annual overhaul on the Laundry Lane slipway at Lowestoft in 1979.

The Customs and Excise patrol vessel *Vigilant* passing through Lowestoft Swing Bridge for her sea trials off the port in 1965.

The 360-ton *Albatross* loading a cargo of chemicals at the North Quay in 1965. She had just joined the Lowestoft-Rotterdam cargo run operated by the East Anglian Shipping Co.

The railway line which once carried fish from the quayside was one of the casualties of a continuing programme of modernisation. This picture was taken in the 1960s.

This Sporting Life

In pursuit of the glittering prizes

WATERSPORTS loom large in the recreational life of the Lowestoft area. Yachtsmen and anglers and powerboat enthusiasts have the choice of pursuing their chosen sports on the open sea or on the more sheltered waters of Oulton Broad and the River Waveney.

But the sporting life of the neighbour-hood also encompasses a wealth of other team and individual pursuits, from the annual hockey and rugby festivals at Easter to tennis, bowls and the great British seasonal pastimes of football and cricket.

And as this selection of photographs demonstrates, there are many other ways in which local people enjoy this sporting life.

Motorcyclists scorching around the scramble course at Herringfleet Hills in 1965.

The summit at last, during another scramble event.

The final of the 70 yards junior hurdles won by Julia Manning, second from right, at the Harris School sports day in 1965.

Spectators watching the long jump event, again at a Harris School Sports day.

A blind bowler preparing to send down a wood at Kensington Gardens, Lowestoft, in 1976 during the annual tournament for blind and partially-sighted people.

Hydroplanes line up in the pits for the start of one of the weekly meetings organised each summer by the Lowestoft and Oulton Broad Motor Boat Club. This event was in August 1976.

Pigeon racing is a popular local pursuit. Pictured here in 1977 is Oulton Broad man Edward Rouse holding a seven-year-old bird which had just returned from the Le Mans race – its 14th Channel crossing.

Young members of the Waveney Gymnastics Club going through their paces in the late 1970s.

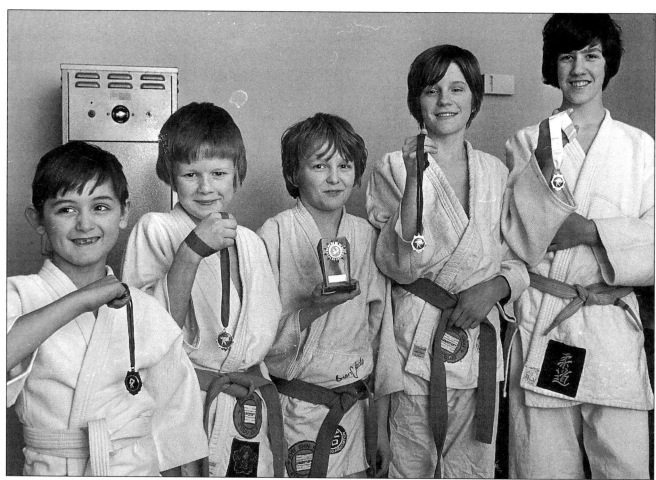

A quintet of proud young judo medal winners from the Kyu Shin Kwai club.

Suffolk champion athletes Sally Jeffries, Mark Gee and Gary High after their championship successes in 1976.

Fifteen-year-old J.Marjoram was runner-up in the Lowestoft junior angling festival at Pakefield in 1977 when he landed this plump 2lb 5½oz codling.

Jimmy Moran leads the Lowestoft Town FC team, the 'Blues', on to the field at the Wellesley Ground in Great Yarmouth in May 1967, for the first leg of their Eastern Counties League Cup Final against close rivals Yarmouth (the 'Bloaters'). Lowestoft won the game in impressive style, 7-3.

It was a fine afternoon in late spring, and pupils of Lowestoft Grammar School were out in force on the playing field to watch the school sports in the mid-1960s.

Motor kart racing, a sport which has enjoyed occasional bursts of popularity in the Lowestoft area, on a grass circuit during the Oulton Broad regatta programme.

Members of the Lake Lothing pub team who were clearly well on target when they faced the camera in the 1960s.

Summer fun at the fete. A donkey derby event provides its share of thrills, and a few spills, at Lowestoft in 1976.

Another season, another reason for keeping fit. Lowestoft Town players being put through a rigorous training stint by new manager Evan Sutherland at the club's Crown Meadow ground in the mid-1970s.

Members of the Harris Middle School soccer team in 1976.

And their counterparts and rivals from Roman Hill School the same season.

Veteran anglers aiming to continue an active role in the sport they loved. Members of the newly-formed Senior Citizens' Angling Club pictured on the South Pier at Lowestoft in the late 1970s.

Oulton Broad FC in determined mood to face the camera in 1950.

Taking a fall. Johnny Yearsley, of Cardiff, wrapped up in the ropes by his opponent, Joe Cornelius, from Bermondsey, during their bout at an open-air wrestling tournament staged at Nicholas Everitt Park, Oulton Broad, in 1965.

A tow home for the outboard hydroplane Do-Do (H.Morrell) after engine trouble had forced him to retire from the first heat of the Daily Mirror Individual Handicap Trophy race at Oulton Broad in 1965.

Racing craft heading at high speed for the next turn at Oulton Broad in 1978.

In the pits. Mechanics and drivers make final adjustments before the British Hydroplane Championship at Oulton Broad in 1979.

Always hopeful. A beach angler casts beyond the surf at Pakefield on a day of strong onshore winds and rough seas in the autumn of 1975.

Trying their utmost. Essex gain possession from a scrum during an inter-county match against Norfolk at Gunton Park, Lowestoft, in 1982.

A reminder that East Anglia is very much a part of the world in which to enjoy traditional country pursuits. Competitors moving to a new position during the Eastern Counties Retriever Society trials on the Somerleyton Estate in 1966.

Top gun. John Bidwell of Oulton Broad, winner of a galaxy of national and world titles for his marksmanship. He is pictured with some of his trophies in 1983.

Well-reefed *Broads One Designs* leaving harbour to face a fresh southerly wind for the Lowestoft Sea Week race at the end of August 1977.

Poetry in motion. *Three Legs of Man 11* lifting her bows from the water as she headed south off Pakefield in the final leg of the Round Britain Race. One of the race stops was at Lowestoft.

Star Lowestoft table tennis player Russell King in action in 1978.

Schoolgirl Anna Smith at the wheel of her racing craft at Oulton Broad in 1981. A number of women drivers have made their mark in the world of powerboat racing.

Members of the Co-op Sports Association badminton section in the 1950-51 season.

The immediate post-war years saw an upsurge of interest in different sports. And cycle speedway on makeshift tracks such as this one at Oulton Broad attracted plenty of daredevil young racers.

They didn't talk much about global warming during the long and bitter winter of 1963. But the frozen waters of Oulton Broad provided an ideal setting for the Broadland sport of ice skating.

Members of Lowestoft Town Cricket Club – whose ground at Denes Oval is the most easterly in the country – pictured during the summer of 1961.

A confusion of motorcyclists in the race for the lead in an event staged at Herringfleet in 1980.

Club president Maurice Hepton drives the first ball to open Lowestoft's new golf course at Rookery Park, Carlton Colville in July 1975.

Three times ladies national freestyle archery champion, Miss Eileen Bucknole of Lowestoft in 1977.

Ever hopeful. Competitors find time to talk about catches of the past, and the fish that sometimes got away, during the annual Pontins fishing week at Pakefield in 1980.

Lowestoft angler Sam Hook with the 32lb cod he caught from the Claremont Pier in 1945 to set a new national record.

Congratulations... and celebrations. Lowestoft Ladies FC – known as The Waves – who were winners of the Women's FA Cup in 1982. They scored a 2-0 win against Cleveland in the Final played at Loftus Road, London. The scorers were Linda Curl and Angie Pretty.

Fish And Ships

The men and the vessels engaged in winning the harvest of the sea

LOWESTOFT remains the country's top fishing port for plaice, although in terms of the number of vessels operating the modern fleet is only a shadow of the past.

The sophisticated beam trawlers of the present are a far cry from the side trawlers of relatively recent times, but the fishermen of Lowestoft are cast in the same sturdy mould as their forefathers.

North Sea fishermen are among the last true hunters, and are called upon to pit their skills against a cruel and unpredictable environment. In that respect nothing has changed since the era of sail and steam.

On shore, some 1,200 people are employed to process and sell the catches. Fish which was once handled on the open quay is now dealt with in a modem processing hall. The pace of change is reflected in this selection of photographs from a market which is very much the home of Fish and Ships.

Grading plaice on the open fish market in 1981.

Filleters at work on the market in January 1978.

A porbeagle shark landed by the trawler *Boston Sea Stallion*. The shark, which eventually went to a Yarmouth seafood restaurant, was bought for just £60 by buyer Michael Cole (right) on behalf of the firm of J.T.Cole.

Another monster catch, a rarely-seen halibut landed in 1981.

A 14ft basking shark was one of the weightier catches of 1976.

The Lowestoft Fisheries Laboratory is one of the major research centres within the European Community. Here Dr G.P.Arnold shows a 2in long acoustic tag of a type being attached to fish in 1976 to chart migratory movements.

Lowestoft's fleet of inshore trawlers tied up in the Hamilton Dock as autumnal gales continued to blow in the North Sea in 1980.

Buyers gather around boxes of fish landed by the inshore fleet in February 1980.

The old open market as it was in the early 1980s.

Repairing nets on board the trawler *Boston Defiant* in 1977.

The stern trawler *Bamby Queen* heading out to sea from her home port.

A young angler tries his luck with a handline from the quay heading as work continues to deal with the morning's catch from the trawler fleet.

Learning the ropes. Trainee fishermen being instructed in netmaking skills in 1965.

Visitors on board the Lowestoft trawler *Scampton*, open to the public in aid of the Royal National Mission to Deep Sea Fishermen, being shown around by former trawlerman William Jarvis in the summer of 1977.

A Lowestoft inshore fishermen at work baiting hundreds of hooks on long lines in the chill January of 1978.

Children from Roman Hill School at Lowestoft pictured during a tour of the quayside as part of their lessons on the fishing industry in 1970.

Inshore fishermen preparing bait for long lines in 1975. Pictured on board the *Children's Friend* are skipper-owner David Cook (centre), his brother Alan (left) and David Esherwood.

The nature of their calling means that fishermen have few opportunities to make their views known to the public ashore. But there was no doubting the sentiments behind this slogan displayed by the beamer *C.K.Amber* in 1980.

The tug *Ness Point* bringing the trawler *Ada Kerby* into harbour in October 1961 after the fishing vessel had broken down with propeller trouble near the Cross Sands lightship.

Skipper Arthur Brinded showing a party of visiting German students some unsold dogfish when he took them on a tour of the fish market in 1976.

A demonstration of fish measuring being given by T.Williams (right) and S.Stevens at a Lowestoft Fisheries Laboratory open day in 1976.

The disabled trawler *Oulton Queen* hard up against the North Extension of the harbour while being brought back to port under tow after running aground on the edge of the Newcome Sands in December 1970.

Final preparations for another trip being made on the deck of a Lowestoft trawler in the spring of 1959.

The skipper of this French trawler, moored alongside the Fishery Protection Vessel *HMS Walton*, was fined £25 and ordered to forfeit his catch for fishing inside the three mile limit in 1961.

Market scavengers. Piratical gulls are always ready to snatch any edible scraps from the day's landings.

Idle trawlers berthed in the trawl basin during a strike by port skippers at the beginning of 1980.

The crew of the Southwold fishing boat *Broadside* cleaning their catch of cod after coming into Lowestoft in January 1983.

Ranks of fish containers provide testimony to the size of catches regarded as commonplace in the 1970s. Indeed, there were no buyers for the plaice seen here and the catch went for fish meal.

Mending the nets aboard the inshore trawler *Semper Crescendo* in 1976.

Inshore vessels
tied up in the
Hamilton Dock.

A market filleter
dealing in expert
fashion with a dogfish,
watched at his work
by children from
Roman Hill School.
The year was 1977.

Lowestoft's quaysides were lined with trawlers at the end of 1967, when the fleet which then comprised more than 100 vessels, remained in port for the Christmas break.

Days of desolation. The old market pictured during the course of demolition to make way for a modern processing hall.

The opening day of the new £10 million market in 1987.

The early morning auction in progress in 1989.

Vessels of the inshore fleet crowded into the Hamilton Dock in 1980.

The trawler *Sailfin* aground at the entrance to Lowestoft harbour in 1965, with the tug *Richard Lee Barber* trying to haul her off.

A catch of 2,700st of cod from the Danish gill netter *Erna Hoy* being auctioned in 1980.

Office staff working a breakfast time shift unloading the trawler *Ripley Queen* after the market lumpers, whose job it would normally have been, stopped work.

A fresh coat of paint for vessels in the inshore fleet in 1975.

It isn't just fish that comes up in the trawl net. Skipper Paul Thomas shows part of an old wooden trawler.

The Silver Darlings

Days when King Herring still reigned

THE prosperity of fishing communities along the East Coast hinged for centuries upon the presence of seemingly inexhaustible shoals of herring. The autumn herring fishery based on Lowestoft and the neighbouring port of Great Yarmouth became, in the course of time, the greatest of its kind in the world, providing food for millions and work to thousands of fishermen and shore workers.

It seemed part of the natural order that the 'Silver darlings' would remain part of the annual bounty of the North Sea.

But within a few short post-war years it became apparent that the herring industry was dying, and that past glories were destined for the history books. The drift net fishery which was a way of life for so many Scottish and English families slipped into extinction.

Now there are only fading memories of the reign of 'King Herring' alongside the

The packed fish hold of the drifter *Faithful II* in 1970 gives an indication of the kind of catches that were once commonplace.

photographic images of a vibrant era in ports such as Lowestoft.

Buyers examine boxes of herring being sold by auction on the Lowestoft market in 1976.

The crew of the West Mersea longshore boat *Swin Ranger* scudding their nets after landing a catch of some 350st of herring in the autumn of 1976.

All hands to the nets. Volunteers helping clear herring from the nets after a longshore boat encountered an unexpectedly large haul close to the beach.

Two of Lowestoft's best known drifter skippers, Ernest (Jumbo) Fiske on the left and George Meen, pictured just before sailing for the herring grounds.

A typical pierhead scene in autumn, with drifters steaming out past the South Pier shortly after World War Two.

Hanging up drift nets on the drying racks on the North Denes in the late 1940s.

Boxes of fresh herring being swung ashore from the drifter *Young Elizabeth* at Lowestoft in 1962.

All hands on deck aboard the Lowestoft drifter *Henrietta Spashett*, landing a catch at her home port in 1960.

Hobson's salesman George Thom selling a catch just landed by the Peterhead vessel *Faithful II* in 1975.

The drifter *Young Elizabeth* heads for the open sea and another night on the herring grounds a few miles off the coast.

Teamwork on the quayside as the catch is brought ashore from the drifter *Margaret Hide*.

A steam drifter's crew landing their catch on the Lowestoft market.

Boxes of herring stacked and ready for sale. Six boxes were the equivalent of the traditional cran measure of some 1,200 fish.

The Prunier Trophy was for many years awarded annually for the biggest catch in a single night during the East Anglian season. Winner when this picture was taken in 1963 was the Small & Co drifter *Norfolk Yeoman*, skippered by Ritson Sims. Pictured at the presentation ceremony are (from left) the Mayor of Lowestoft, Charles Ramm; the chairman of the English Herring Catchers' Association, Fred Catchpole; Skipper Ritson Sims and Tony Cartwright of Small & Co.

Landing the previous night's catch during the home fishing.

Skipper George Draper (centre), twice a Prunier Trophy winner, discussing his plans for the night's fishing with ship's husband and boat owner Eddie Beamish (left) and drifter owner Fred Catchpole.

A weary but contented smile from Jack Hale, skipper of the Lowestoft inshore boat *Seafarer*, during the landing of a big catch.

Expert eyes examine the first catch of herring at the start of a new season at Lowestoft in 1967. The Fraserburgh drifter *Fertile*, skippered by Andrew Tait, had put ashore a catch of 41 cran.

The herring industry was in decline in the 1950s, but good catches were still to be had. This landing was being put ashore by the local drifter *Merbreeze*.

Longshore boats lined up at Pakefield in 1970 in readiness for the next suitable tide.

A Scots drifter entering Lowestoft harbour during the 1960 season.

Canning at the former Morton's factory at Lowestoft not long after World War Two.

The Duke of Edinburgh examines the Prunier Trophy during a visit to the Lowestoft and East Suffolk Maritime Society museum at Sparrow's Nest in 1978. With him is the Society's chairman, Roy French.

Tools of the trade. Ted Frost (right), former shipwright and author of a classic book on the building of wooden drifters, *From Tree to Sea*, showing a cooper's plane to fellow members of the Maritime Society, Mr D.Adams (left) and Mr C.Chipperfield.

With their nets spread on deck after a morning's fishing, these longshore boats rest at their berths in the Hamilton Dock in the mellow afternoon sunshine in 1967.

The Changing Scene

Here yesterday and gone today

NEW roads and new shops, out of town supermarkets and urban pedestrian precincts are all part of the changing scene. Sometimes it is hard to remember the way in which things looked just a few years back, so complete is the transformation.

Newspapers are able to serve as journals of record in this respect, showing us what we have lost and what we have gained in the name of progress.

Who now remembers the names of the 13 pubs which once served the Beach area of Lowestoft? Or can picture St John's Church on the site which is now the Levington Court housing development?

Who, indeed, can easily recall the days when the main A12 traffic clogged London Road North and there was no pedestrian area in the heart of town?

Horses and riders trek across part of the former golf course at Lowestoft in 1978 before the start of development to transform the area into an 'urban village'.

The Beach area of Lowestoft, with the process of industrialisation already well advanced when this picture was taken in 1966.

Sculpt William Redgrave with his statue of a fisherman, *The Call of the Sea*, after its unveiling at Station Square in 1980.

The Duchess of Kent the opening of the new divisional fire headquarters at Lowestoft in 1972.

Work in progress enlarging the ballroom of the Royal Hotel in 1960. The extension offered seating for over 500 for banquets but now both the ballroom and the main hotel have gone, and the site is occupied by Royal Green and the East Point Pavilion.

Another bucket of concrete being lowered to the bed of Mutford Lock, the link between Oulton Broad and the sea during rebuilding after the collapse of the North Wall in 1964.

Another transformation scene. The old North Extension of the harbour being developed as an offshore construction base for SLP in 1980.

A Dutch dredger at work widening the bridge channel at Lowestoft in 1980 to permit larger vessels to use the harbour.

Gale cones at the Coastguard lookout which formerly stood at the seaward end of Hamilton Road, and has now been demolished. This picture was taken in 1980.

The end of the Odeon Cinema in London Road North. The building came down in 1979 to make way for the present Britten Centre.

Clearing the site for the new Lowestoft divisional police headquarters in 1975.

The end of another local cinema. The scene after a devastating blaze which wrecked the Palace cinema in Royal Thoroughfare in 1966.

The North Sea is constantly at work seeking to undermine defences. Major repair work was called for in 1975 after the winter storms had damaged the North Wall.

An isolated railway arch juts out from a North Suffolk field during clearance work on embankments along the former Lowestoft-Yarmouth line in 1981.

Once the headquarters of the local branch of the RSPCA, and in another incarnation the headquarters of Lowestoft Constituency Labour Party, this substantial building was one of many to disappear as part of successive road improvement schemes.

Demolition work in progress on old buildings at Sparrow's Nest in 1963. Remaining premises alongside now house a popular cafe and two museums, the Lowestoft War Memorial Museum and that of the Royal Naval Patrol Service which was based at the Nest during World War Two.

Normanston House falling to the demolition crews in 1963 during a decade when Lowestoft and many other towns lost hundreds of fine buildings to clearance programmes.

Old cottages in High Street being cleared in 1964.

Old Nelson Street in 1973 before major redevelopment brought the disappearance of these pantiled cottages.

These houses in Duke's Head Street were among the oldest in Lowestoft. But age did not spare them from the bulldozer in 1965.

Old houses in the Beach area of Lowestoft in 1964.

The former Morton's canning factory in Belveder Road, another of the companies which once offered work to hundreds of local people.

The little pavilion which was originally built for the Royal Norfolk & Suffolk Yacht Club was removed plank by plank to the Crown Meadow football ground in 1903 – and was still going strong when this picture was taken in 1968.

The Suffolk Hotel has long since been swept away and this corner of Lowestoft is now the setting for a McDonald's restaurant.

Once a favourite haunt of local fisherman, the Stone Cottage was one of a number of Lowestoft pubs to disappear in redevelopment schemes.

One of the last of a number of properties demolished to make way for new housing in the St Peter's Street area of the town's old market was Dowson's bakery, pictured here in defiant style amid the surrounding redevelopment in 1967.

Empty buildings, no matter what their purpose, sadly attract the attention of vandals in the course of time. This was the scene inside the former St John's Church in 1977.

The last gas lamps in Lowestoft were still to be seen in Lighthouse Score in the late 1960s.

Local children form a salvage team collecting useful bits of timber during demolition of the Gas House Tavern in the 1960s.

Built in 1929 to serve the new Alliance Artificial Silk Works, this 80ft water tower was finally demolished in 1967.

Down with the old and up with the new. The St Peter's Court multi-storey block of flats taking shape against the 1960s skyline.

The South Pier Pavilion, now demolished, pictured under construction in 1955.

Up Against The Elements

Days when it wasn't all wine and roses

THE sun does not always shine, and the vulnerable coastline of East Anglia is hit by more than its share of winter tempests. Heavy snow is relatively rare, but the people of Lowestoft are hardened to the effects of that 'lazy' north-easterly wind which comes straight from Siberia and makes itself felt through the thickest and warmest clothing. Summer visitors rightly expect to enjoy the sparkling best of the seaside weather but there have been days even at the peak of the season when thunderstorms have been known to gather with impressive, though thankfully short-lived effect.

Here are a few reminders of days which are only a distant memory when we are basking in the warm sun.

The thatched cottage at the entrance to Belle Vue Park is a setting which attracts countless artists and photographers. Since this picture was taken after a March snowfall in 1962 the cottage has been gutted by fire, and restored to its original state.

Another chilly day, this time in early 1959, with a path being broken through the ice at Oulton Broad.

Iced up: On board the Lowestoft research vessel *Clione* during the bitter winter of 1963.

Hardly a winter wonderland, but a town centre scene showing that public transport has sometimes been able to keep going when car drivers have been happy to stay at home.

Lowestoft youngsters making the most of the snow as they scamper across the Ravine bridge which joins North Parade and Belle Vue Park.

The landing stage near the yacht club at Nicholas Everitt Park, Oulton Broad, was twisted out of shape by the action of thick ice in the winter of 1963.

The process of coastal erosion shown to dramatic effect when this well shaft was exposed by cliff falls at Covehithe, just south of Lowestoft. The brickwork soon collapsed as the sea continued its relentless advance.

A wartime blockhouse at Benacre proved no defence against the power of the North Sea.

Homeward bound. Lowestoft lifeboat returning to harbour after another rescue mission.

Spray sends a cascade of foam shooting high into the air as another wave breaks against the Esplande at Lowestoft.

Rough seas pound the South Pier during a storm in the 1970s.

After the storm: Beachcombers keeping watch for coins left exposed by the receding tide on the South Beach.

The upturned bows of the tanker *Eleni V* off Lowestoft in 1978, with the tug *Scotsman* holding the wreck in position. This sinking caused extensive oil pollution along miles of beaches.

Workmen up to their knees in thick glutinous oil during clearance work on the North Beach after the *Eleni V* disaster.

There was a ready response from local people when volunteers were asked to help clear the oil from the *Eleni V*. Young members of the newly-formed Waveney branch of Friends of the Earth were among those who went into action on the North Beach. Pictured front are (left to right) Penny and Charlotte Forsyth, Anne Dick and Mary Davies.

Fishermen were badly hit by the *Eleni V* disaster. Skipper Mick Whittingstall of the inshore trawler *Corina* examines an oil-polluted net.

High winds in the spring of 1965 brought down this 350-year-old beech tree alongside Benacre Church. Branches brushed the main porch but the church itself escaped damage. Foresters from the Benacre estate were quickly in action cutting up the tree.

Another casualty of the storm. This unoccupied caravan at the Azure Seas site in Corton Woods was badly damaged when a big fir tree was brought down in an October gale in 1976.

This shed finished up on an outhouse roof during a storm which swept the area in January 1976.

Left: It must clear up soon. Visitors to a regatta fete at Oulton Broad sit it out during a torrential summer downpour.

Below: Four members of the Essex Hydroplane Club determined to keep their heads dry during a rainstorm in August 1976.

Bottom: While their parents cleared up the mess after the storm which flooded the North Denes camping site in 1976, young visitors found a new attraction in the pools of water outside their tents.

Subscribers

Malcolm F Andrews
Miss J A Bailey
Mike Barnard
Mrs Sarah Barnes
G E Bellward
Paul Belton
Mr T H Betts
J W Bond
Mrs Joyce C G Bradnick
Richard D C Bradnick
Nicholas & Trixie Brighouse
Mr D J Bullard
Terry Bullen
Keith Burrows
Leonard Charles Butcher
Emma Louisa Button (née Welch)
Mr & Mrs I C Carter
Mr & Mrs L A Carter
Mr John Clarke
Pauline & Len Cook
Brenda Critoph
Mrs J N Creed
Fred Dunham
S Earl
Mr Stephen Kenneth Edwards
Chris Eyers
Mr Andrew Fiske
Mrs Ruth Ford (née Eade) WB
Diane Girling
Robin Gooch
D G Gosling
Colin Grimmer
Mr Alan G Hales
Heather Hampton
Mrs M G Harvey
Mr Gerald E Hogg
Graham C Holmes
Simon T Hurn
Barbara James
Stuart Jones
Mrs J Hurren
P C B Kent
Mr P J Killby
P C Kirk
S A Kirk

Mark Andrew Larter & Peter Frederick Larter
Derek Lilley
Barbara McKie
Terry & Diana Mason
Austin Mobbs
Mr Henry Granville Moore
Mr David Morgan
Mr Raymond Nobbs
Stanley J Nobbs
R H Norman
D G Oldman
Anthony Peek
F J Pilcher
David Porter MP
A Powley
Mrs Kathleen Price
Charles Pryce
David Pryce
James Pryce
Elizabeth Rafferty
Gordon & Dorothy Reynolds
C L Rice
P Rice
Robert D J Roach
Dennis Edward Rouse
Mrs E A Ruck (Liz)
Ronald G Sampson
Barrie David Sandham
Mr Don Sansom
Mr G W Short
M J Smith
Brian Soloman
Margaret Tabor
Pam & Philip Tovell
Jennifer & John Tucker
J W Turner
Mrs A Webster
Mr & Mrs M Whitaker
R J White
Mrs Ethel Willes
Fred & Rose Willis
Mr Leonard J Woods
P D Vincent
Carolyn Youngs